F HORN

CONCERT FAVORITES

Volume 2

Band Arrangements Correlated with Essential Elements Band Method Book 1

ISBN 978-1-4234-0083-7

HAL•LEONARD®

7777 W. BLUEMOUND RD. P.O. BOX 13819 MILWAUKEE, WI 53213

00860171

BANDROOM BOOGIE

F HORN

MICHAEL SWEENEY

Copyright © 2000 by HAL LEONARD CORPORATION
International Copyright Secured   All Rights Reserved

BEETHOVEN'S NINTH

HORN

LUDWIG VAN BEETHOVEN
Arranged by PAUL LAVENDER

0860171

GALLANT MARCH

F HORN

MICHAEL SWEENEY

00860171

HIGH ADVENTURE

HORN

PAUL LAVENDER

ROCK & ROLL – PART II
(The Hey Song)

F Horn

Words and Music b
MIKE LEANDER and GARY GLITTE
Arranged by PAUL LAVENDE

00860171

AMAZING GRACE

HORN

Traditional American Melody
Arranged by PAUL LAVENDER

0860171

F HORN

INFINITY
(Concert March)

JAMES CURNOW (ASCAP)

00860171

LATIN FIRE

HORN

JOHN HIGGINS

LINUS AND LUCY

F HORN

By VINCE GUARALDI
Arranged by MICHAEL SWEENEY

(From The Paramount Motion Picture STAR TREK GENERATIONS)

THEME FROM "STAR TREK® GENERATIONS"

HORN

Music by DENNIS McCARTHY
Arranged by MICHAEL SWEENEY

AMERICAN SPIRIT MARCH

F HORN

JOHN HIGGINS

GATHERING IN THE GLEN

HORN

MICHAEL SWEENEY

THE LOCO-MOTION

Words and Music by
GERRY GOFFIN and CAROLE KING
Arranged by JOHN HIGGINS

F HORN

00860171

ROYAL FIREWORKS MUSIC

GEORGE FREDERIC HANDEL
Arranged by MICHAEL SWEENEY

HORN

0860171

SCARBOROUGH FAIR

F HORN

Traditional English
Arranged by JOHN MOSS

Cantabile Moderato